Ancestral Intelligence

ALSO BY VERA SCHWARCZ

Colors of Veracity: A Search for Truth in China, and Beyond (forthcoming, University of Hawaii Press)

Brief Rest in the Garden of Flourishing Grace (Red Heifer Press, 2009)

The Chisel of Remembrance (Antrim House, 2009)

Place and Memory in the Singing Crane Garden (University of Pennsylvania Press, 2008)

Truth is Woven (Premier Poets Series #31, Newport, Rhode Island, 2005)

In the Garden of Memory, with Chava Pressburger (March Street Press, 2004)

A Scoop of Light—Poems (March Street Press, 2000)

Fresh Words for a Jaded World—Selected Poems (Blue Feather Press, 2000)

Bridge Across Broken Time: Chinese and Jewish Cultural Memory (Yale University Press, 1998)

Time for Telling Truth is Running Out: Conversations with Zhang Shenfu (Yale University, 1992)

The Chinese Enlightenment: The Legacy of the May Fourth Movement in Modern China (University of California, Berkeley Press, 1986)

Ancestral Intelligence

Renditions and Poems

Vera Schwarcz

Antrim House

Simsbury, Connecticut

Library of Congress Control Number: 2013939214

ISBN: 978-1-936482-49-8

Printed & bound by United Graphics, Inc.

First Edition, 2013

Book Design by Rennie McQuilkin

Front cover design by Andy Youlieguo Zhou

Logograph designs by Aiai Chen

Author Photograph by John Wareham

Antrim House
860.217.0023
AntrimHouse@comcast.net
www.AntrimHouseBooks.com
21 Goodrich Road, Simsbury, CT 06070

To my grandchildren

who keep renewing the ancestors
more intelligently and more lovingly
than I ever thought possible

Acknowledgements

I wish to thank the editors of journals in which earlier versions of these poems have appeared—*Cha: An Asian Literary Journal, Confluences: The Journal of Graduate Liberal Studies, Plainsongs, Bridges, Connecticut River Review, Ellipsis, Resonance* and *Blue Unicorn.*

The poems in this work could not have taken shape without the help of Chinese friends and research assistants. From the very start of my writing about Chen Yinke, I felt deeply intimidated by his scholarship and literary verve. As an outsider to the Chinese tradition, how could I possibly step onto a terrain that has baffled many distinguished scholars from within? Then, I received a phone call from one of the world experts on Chen Yinke and Chinese history—Professor Yu Yingshi, Professor Emeritus at Princeton University. He had called to say some kind words about my previous book, *Place and Memory in Singing Crane Garden*. I mentioned to him that I was thinking of writing about Chen Yinke but that I felt inadequate to the task. In his vivacious Chinese, he told me: "You can and you must!"

Professor Yu's own annotations of Chen's poems have helped me understand many difficult allusions. And my young Chinese research assistants at Wesleyan University worked with me to decode each line, word by word. They not only saved me dozens of hours with a dictionary, but also encouraged the project as a whole. Their interest in the life of this poet-historian confirmed my own sense that his themes apply beyond China. Yang Guangshuo worked on many poems with me and also prepared a PowerPoint presentation, which I was able to use in China, Israel and this country as I began to present the project in more public forums. In addition, Sharon Li and Rain Xie helped with literal translations upon which I developed the renditions in the first part of this volume.

Aiai Chen, a fine calligrapher and skilled researcher, added grace and intellectual depth to this book. The three characters for "wound" (*shang*), "writing" (*xie*) and "old" (*jiu*) executed by her brush appear at various points in the book. She also located various logographs in ancient etymological sources, thereby enriching each poem with connotations erased in the Mao era.

Andy Youlieguo Zhou, a brilliant graphic designer and historian, has been a constant interlocutor in the evolution of this project. At the very end, as I decided on the title *Ancestral Intelligence*, he found a most vivid way to convey this theme for a front cover image: he created a brash version of the simplified *ling* that captures the avaricious energy of Maoist China. Broken bits of the older, fuller *ling* show through the red, bearing witness to the survival of a shattered tradition inside the very structure that denies its aesthetic claims. He also provided digital versions of the classic and modern logographs that appear in Part II of the book. For that too I am eternally grateful.

Finally, I want to thank Rennie McQuilkin of Antrim House, my editor for this second volume of poems. Not only did he give me the idea of seeing Chen Yinke as a "Chinese Tiresias," but he was also an animated conversation partner in discussing all aspects of the logograph poems. He knew, long before I was sure, that the two sets of poems in this book belong together and that they can be made to speak to readers who are not China specialists. My gratitude to his ear and his pencil marks will endure long after this work is finished.

TABLE OF CONTENTS

A RELUCTANT RESCUER OF WORDS

In dark times, the warmth that is the pariah's substitute for light exerts a great fascination upon all who are so ashamed of the world as it is that they would like to take refuge in invisibility.... The poet and the historian have the task of setting the process of narration in motion and of involving us in it.

Hannah Arendt, "On Humanity in Dark Times"

This book is about language as a life raft in times of historical darkness. It brings together poems based upon the tragic life of historian Chen Yinke (1890-1969) with verses focused upon single Chinese logographs which have been deformed during the last century of political turmoil. Although rooted deeply in East Asian traditions, these poems are not intended for academic specialists. Rather, my aim has been to reach all those who empathize with Hannah Arendt's reflections on meanings of humaneness in times of inhumanity.[1] Arendt understood that words, much like individual persons, can be subjected to brutal persecution in the name of a so-called common good. This volume counters that ravage by paying tribute to spiritual and linguistic resilience. These verses are meant to map a landscape of beauty, grace and truth that will outlast the machinations of destructive revolutionaries in China and beyond.

The two segments of this book evolved over a decade of research and poetic revision. At first, I simply dared myself to put one toe into the ocean of scholarship that surrounded the life of a single eminent intellectual known mostly inside China. Later, I found myself transformed by the depth of suffering which tested the integrity of men and women who live through dark times. The theme of historical trauma had threaded itself through my previous works about modern China as well as through three collections of poems about my parents' experience during the Holocaust in Europe. The dilemmas of memory were familiar to me before I wrote these poems. Here, I sought something different: to paint with words the maiming and the triumph of language itself.

Chen Yinke (1890-1969) was an ideal subject for my meditations upon the destruction and survival of linguistic traditions. As a renowned historian and poet, he was skilled at describing as well as mourning the ravage that became my broader concern. The poems in the first section of this book risk undue modernization by borrowing

Chen's voice to speak to a Western audience. This risk, I believe, was worth taking. My aim in creating my "renditions" of Chen Yinke's poems was to extract and to transpose into a contemporary idiom the essence of Chen's grief.

These renditions, which comprise the first section of this book, are not translations. They are based very loosely upon Chen Yinke's occasional jottings, few of which were published during his lifetime. From posthumous compilations and memoirs, I pieced together this vision of a man who never tired of rescuing endangered words. Using Chen's voice allowed me to explore how each utterance has the potential to revive culture, especially in times and places where the prospects for authentic speech appear bleakest.

Renditions based on Chen Yinke's life led me quite naturally to the "logograph poems" in the second half of this volume. While researching the dense historical allusions in Chen's writing, I started to seek out the etymology of older forms in Chinese language. Many of these words (and ideas) had been simplified during the reign of Mao Zedong. The result was a tragic desiccation of the emotional and intellectual landscape which mirrored Chen's experiences. By recovering the fullness of the ancients' speech I wanted to provide a new angle of vision for Western readers who do not know Chinese. Hannah Arendt's description of survivors of atrocity grew more vivid in my mind as I wrote these poems about ideograms deformed but not degutted by China's Communist regime.

The willful flattening of a cultural terrain is not China's tragedy alone. Our global society as a whole suffers from corruption and materialism. Therefore, I believe, even a single pariah's enduring integrity has the power to awaken us to the possibility of countering corrosive authorities at home and abroad. As a German refugee from the Holocaust, Hannah Arendt understood this power and chose to address a passionate plea to poets and historians to start the process of salvaging voices of conscience for posterity. This volume is but a small stepping stone on that road. The poems based on the life of Chen Yinke explore layers of loss beyond one man's suffering during the Cultural Revolution. Similarly, each Chinese word that sparked verses about logographs is used to enhance the richness of expression possible though "ancestral intelligence." This, I discovered, depends upon an intimate and nuanced communication with a past which outweighs sterile shards of speech all too prevalent today.

China's Tiresias

Diminutive in stature, blind and crippled at the time of his death in 1969, Chen Yinke towers ever taller over China's literary landscape. In an era of economic prosperity riddled by intellectual mediocrity and thwarted freedom of expression, his quiet courage is endlessly prized. There are more and more books, documentaries and conferences dedicated to Chen's memory—as if in honoring his independence of spirit, Chinese intellectuals can palpate virtues still viewed with suspicion by the Communist regime. These memorials often center upon Chen's enduring integrity in times of political persecution. One photograph from 1959 is particularly inspiring for Chen Yinke's admirers. It shows the aged, infirm scholar at his home in Canton, just as he was beginning to be victimized during a Maoist campaign against overly scrupulous historical scholarship. No photographer is named and no caption provided. Instead, the fierce gaze of the old man speaks volumes wordlessly.

Chen Yinke confronts political adversity with clenched lips and a firm hand on his blind man's cane. His attackers used the Maoist slogan *Thicken the present, thin out the past* to condemn him for an "excessive attachment to historical scholarship and literary studies."[2] Demoted and sightless, Chen continued his writing with the aid of research assistants and his devoted wife. It was only the din of violence and terror during the Cultural Revolution that finally silenced the voice of this thoroughly un-Maoist historian-poet.

Chen Yinke's moral courage and persistence were, quite literally, rooted in ancestral intelligence. Born into a prominent family of scholar officials in the last decade of the 19th Century, Chen carried the pain of cultural decay and imperial politics in his bones. His grandfather, Chen Baozhen (1831-1900), had been a high level Confucian official in the Qing dynasty government. Having served as provincial governor of Hunan, he became a supporter of reformers who argued for constitutional monarchy in 1898. As a result, the Empress Dowager Cixi forced him to commit suicide as soon as she returned to power in autumn of 1900. Chen's own father, Chen Sanli (1852-1937), also took the risk of expressing pro-reform views, for which he suffered exile and persecution in Japan. Disenchanted with politics altogether, this gentleman-scholar turned to the project of new poetry in the 20th Century, never imagining that his offspring would take art and scholarship in directions going far beyond Confucian self-cultivation.

Chen Yinke's older brother, Chen Hengke (1876-1923) used the studio name of Shi Zheng (Master of the Past) and went on to become one of the best known modern painters of the 20th Century. Chen Yinke followed him to Japan, but more as a researcher than an artist. It was the scholar's brush that attracted the diminutive younger brother, who went on to deepen his linguistic studies in Berlin, Zurich and Paris. In these centers of global learning, Chen Yinke continued to absorb fully—but never foolishly—the spirit of enlightenment that animated his generation.

"New culture" was the favorite slogan of the young men and women who went to study abroad in the 1910s. From foreign universities, they argued for language and literary reform with increasingly radical implications. Unlike this cohort, Chen Yinke took time to study and master nine foreign languages—among them Japanese, English, French, German, Sanskrit, and Persian, as well as Mongolian, Tibetan, Greek, Latin, Tangut and Turkic (which he later put to good use in his studies of the sinification of Buddhist institutions in China). No wonder that a contemporary Chinese historian characterized Chen Yinke as "the most sophisticated mind in 20th Century China." [3]

Whereas other modernist intellectuals dabbled a bit in Western literature in order to attack traditional Chinese cultural values, Chen Yinke explored both in depth. For Chen and his colleagues, Ibsen was one of the Western writers who became a handy icon in the effort to affirm a new sense of individualism. In 1918, the well known philosopher and writer Hu Shi wrote an impassioned plea entitled "The Ibsenism in My Heart." This was the start of a process that made an "ism" out of each new idea that Chinese students stumbled upon in their studies abroad.[4] In contrast to such modernist theorizers, Chen took a long, difficult boat journey to Ibsen's burial place in Norway, and there penned one of his earliest poems (improvised here as "Midnight Sun") describing a passionate hope for the revival of China's literary tradition.

At Harvard in the late 1910s and upon his return to China in 1925, Chen Yinke continued his explorations of a new Chinese literature in the company of classicists such as Wu Mi (1894-1978) and Wang Guowei (1877-1927). These older mentors recognized the young man's scholarly brilliance and linguistic agility. As soon as he returned from abroad, they invited him to be part of the founding of a new institute dedicated to National Studies (Guo Xue) in Beijing's Qinghua University. Here, Chen flourished as an intellectual. Here, too, he met and married Tang Yun (1893-1969), the extraordinarily gifted daughter of another well-known Confucian scholar-official. In Beijing in the 1920s, Chen Yinke also began to suffer from the aggressive reticular degeneration that would bring about his blindness in the 1940s.

The suicide of Wang Guowei in 1927 added a fresh layer of grief to the life of Chen Yinke. The news of Wang's death shocked the entire intellectual community in China, but no one took it to heart as deeply as his disciple, Chen. Other scholars rushed to attribute the violent end of China's foremost literary scholar to personal intrigues, political conservatism, and the malaise characteristic of "bourgeois elites."[5] Chen Yinke, by contrast, delved into the ethical and cultural values that had sustained Wang and that were becoming less and less viable in China's public life. My renditions depicting Chen's response to the suicide of Wang Guowei aim to capture the impact of a mentor who had hoped to salvage truth and genuine scholarship for modern China. The loftiness of this ambition (expressed in a poem that I have entitled "The Culture of Our Divine Land") stands in stark contrast to the "whimper of odious crows"—Chen Yinke's own metaphor for the babble of public intellectuals fawning upon various warlords all over China.

This personal outcry was very different from the public eulogy that Chen was finally persuaded to write for Wang Guowei in 1929.

Qinghua University needed some words to honor this renowned teacher, but Chen wanted to continue howling in an inwardly authentic voice. The compromise was a text that I have reworked into a rendition entitled "Carved in Black Alabaster." The formal eulogy was eventually inscribed in stone. My poem, on the other hand, gives voice to Chen's privately expressed fears that his own voice would eventually become hostage to China's chilling "eternity."

Eternity looked especially grim in the late 1920s and 1930s as the Nationalist regime of Jiang Kai-shek kept murdering Communists while Japan attacked and eventually conquered most of China. Chen's disgust with all this politicking shows through in poetic jottings as well as his eager acceptance of an invitation to take a Chair in Chinese history at Oxford. The journey out of war-torn China was not an easy or a short one. It took Chen Yinke first to Kunming in the southwest, then to Hong Kong and back again to Chengdu in Siquan province. Finally, when he made it to England in 1945, it was not to teach at Oxford but to try one more operation for his badly deteriorating eyes. One of the best surgeons in London handed down a bleak verdict: there was nothing to be done to reverse Chen's reticular degeneration. He would have to live with rapidly approaching blindness.

This journey away from his wife and three young daughters left Chen Yinke deeply dispirited. On the boat back from England, he wrote about a crushing loneliness and the vanishing world of books. The companions of his soul were slipping further and further into a cursed darkness. It was during these years before the Communist victory in 1949, that Chen took on (almost unwittingly) the role of China's Tiresias.[6] Although the trauma of becoming blind was at first personal, one unseeing man soon began to fight against a wider sort of blindness undermining his family and culture.

Blinded before he turned 60, Chen began to hear more keenly than other men. Like the blind Greek prophet of Thebes, Chen too glimpsed the failure of the gods. It was not just the outbreak of civil war in China that hounded the mind of this sightless scholar. It was the oncoming ravage of culture and ethics that he was powerless to stop. One my renditions that seeks to capture his grief is titled "No One to Rescue Words." Based upon verses that Chen Yinke penned on his 56th birthday, this poem elaborates the vision of a blind scholar listening for each word carried off the pages of his beloved books by tunneling worms. The verses upon which the poem is based did not express simply a personal sorrow. They were meant as a warning to China's culture as whole.

Chen's prophetic grief is also evident in a poem that I have called "Unbearably Verdant." This work comes from jottings composed throughout 1947 and 1948, as civil war engulfed north China. Chen Yinke had returned to Beijing, only to find a devastated city where warring authorities left no room for any cherishing of landscape or culture. The transliteration and literal translation of one of Chen's poems from this period is as follows:

cong cong jia qi gu you zhou—
(bursting, bursting beautiful air ancient secluded city)
ce shi chong lai lei bu shou—
(severed world again return tears don't harvest)
tao guan yi fei qian duo shu—
(peach vistas already not before extent tress)
gao jie fan shi zui gao lou
(stalk street overturned stands most tall building)
ming yuan bei jian kong duo shi
(famous garden north supervision emptied many scholars)
lao fu dong cheng you du you
(old man eastern city has solitary worries)
chou chang nian nian mian shi di
(disconsolate melancholy recall sleep eat places)
yi chun can meng shang xin tou
(single spring barbarous dream arouses heart-mind) [7]

Chen Yinke's original lines follow the classical seven-character pattern and often play with internal rhymes. They are also filled with historical allusions, especially to the end of the Tang dynasty when nomadic invaders were threatening the capital city of Chang'an. Those familiar with Beijing's history in the 1940s would also recognize his reference to "Stalk Street" (guo jie) as the site favored by foreign envoys to the Guomindang government.

My own rendition leaves out these dense allusions while drawing upon the bleak mood of that period. It is also informed by the discovery that Chen was especially fond of a novel about an aged acrobat during the reign of Tang Xuanzong. This narrative ends with the old man complaining about youths who have the heart of "northern nomads." That expression gave me the last line I needed to convey

Chen's prophetic anticipation of the Red Guards who would roam the streets of China mercilessly in the 1960s.

In 1948-49, however, this vision was still a vague one. As the Communists hurtled toward victory, Chen Yinke could have fled from his homeland. Several high-placed Nationalist colleagues offered him airplane tickets and other exit routes out of Communist China. Chen refused them all. Eventually, he left Beijing with a broken heart and moved to Canton to make his home at Sun Yatsen University. He chose an enduring connection to the cultural legacy of his native land over the freedom to pursue his own scholarly muse.

As a blind and ever alert witness to the new regime's atrocities, Chen became more prophetic than he had ever meant to be. His personal calling had been that of the scholar who also tried to create an island of peace for his family, complete with nights of drinking wine and listening to cicadas with his wife. These joys became increasingly curtailed. In 1953, academic authorities in Beijing invited Chen Yinke to come north again and serve as director of the newly founded Institute of History housed inside the Soviet style Academy of Social Sciences. Chen's answer was as shocking as it was admirable: he would accept only if he was excused from all political study and Marxist theorizing, and China's top Communist party authorities agreed to write a letter confirming this agreement.[8] Needless to say, no letter came and Chen remained in the South, where his refusal to tow the party line was overlooked, for a while. It is only retrospectively that Chen Yinke's courage and integrity have begun to shine like a bright moon over China's intellectually denuded landscape. In the 1950s and 1960s, most other scholars and writers chose perforce to bend with the winds of Maoist orthodoxy. The more they bent, the more one lonely old man's resistance gained meaning and the force of inspiration.

Common Folks Become Murderous

The image of Chen Yinke that dominates the moral landscape of post-Mao China was forged in the crucible of the Cultural Revolution (1966-1976). Looking back at those scorching years, contemporary scholars are riveted by Chen's independence of mind. One of the first books to detail Chen's tragedy as well as his ethical triumph was Lu Jiandong's 1997 study entitled *The Last Twenty Years of Chen*

Yinke's Life.[9] With its black cover showing a solitary thinker gripping his cane (an intentionally gloomy extraction of Chen's face out of a family photograph taken in the early 1950s), Lu detailed all the persecutions heaped upon China's foremost scholar until his cruel death in 1969. This was clearly a parable about the larger suffering of China's educated elites under the Maoist regime. Yet this larger message had to remain veiled, since China was in the grip of another decade of repression and enforced amnesia following the bloody crackdown in Tiananmen Square in June, 1989.

Writing about Chen Yinke's personal integrity thus became way to hint at other key virtues that remained unspeakable and unlivable in Communist China. In Chinese, "integrity" is called *qijie*. This is a concept that harks back to centuries of Confucian self-cultivation during many repressive dynasties. It was not just the Communist party that had sought to break men of truth. Emperors and their minions had tried to do the same, again and again. In response, poets and painters adopted the symbol of wind-swept bamboo to convey the tribulations of men of conscience during inimical times.[10] Despite chilling storms that decimate greening branches, the knots of old bamboo grow stronger, just as the determination to bear witness to *qijie* becomes more fierce in the face of political persecution.

Chen Yinke embodied this kind of witnessing throughout the 1950s and 1960s. While other intellectuals retained a sliver of hope that Mao Zedong would open up the gates of freedom for thought and art during the Hundred Flowers Movement of 1956-57, the blind and increasingly isolated Chen heard a darker chant. Poems from that period—improvised here as "Cawing" and "A Prisoner of Rush-Leaf Swords"—record his darkening mood. Like Tiresias, Chen listened to bird songs as an augury. Instead of orioles and larks, he heard the deafening chatter of politicians, the shrill arias of false heroes, and the coming clang of iron chains. Privately jotted poetic musings, he knew, were doing little more than paving the way to his own beheading.

The only solace in this cacophony of repression was his research into the life and death of the late Ming dynasty courtesan, Liu Rushi (1618-1664). Chen Yinke had written about famous women before. What was new in this project was the unashamed identification of the blind old man with a prostitute of an earlier era who had tried to save the culture of her homeland on the eve of the Manchu invasion. Chen's decade-long work on *The Unofficial Biography of Liu Rushi* was carried out with the aid of research assistants; and when these left out of fear or political persecution, with the help of his highly literate wife.

This was a project of immense personal interest, gaining momentum precisely during the years in which Chen first came under direct attack by the Communist party in 1958-59. Demoted, ill, permanently crippled after a fall in the bathtub, Chen Yinke continued to work, all along knowing that his book could never be published on the Chinese mainland. Using Liu's poetry as a gateway into a world in which classical values tottered on the brink of extinction, Chen found a way of giving voice to his own concerns. As one scholar noted, the biography of Liu Rushi, "leads readers ultimately into a landscape of graveyards and ruins... With the aid of philological work and treating poetry as a record of ephemeral moments, Chen Yinke attempted to hear the voices of silence which filled a void that was centuries old."[11]

"Voices of silence" became a leitmotif for many of the renditions I have written about Chen's life in the 1960s. First, I sought to express the poet's identification with Liu Rushi in a poem entitled "Mourning for Language and Land." That moment of scholarly satisfaction was followed by the harshest years endured by Chen Yinke and his wife, Tang Yun. Again, as in the 1940s and 1950s, Chen turned out to be exquisitely attuned to the unsayable and to the unsaid. He began to hear the screams of death long before they were unleashed by Mao Zedong's Red Guards in 1966. As soon as he had finished his book on Liu Rushi, Chen Yinke began to view himself as a doomed man. Each new year celebrated at the time of the chilly spring festival brought him gloomy divinations of the terror to come. When the ocean of Red slogans washed up directly on the doorsteps of his house, he must have been spiritually prepared.

Yet nothing in the previous auguries of China's Tiresias had prepared him for the violence of the attacks unleashed from 1967 through 1969. It was one thing to imagine oneself as doomed to death. It was quite another reality to face a mob with murder in the eyes. The blind old man grew sicker and more depressed. At first, the Red Guards shouted slogans outside his gate, accusing him of every conceivable "bourgeois crime." Their brutal speech was a violation of Chen's soul and became my subject in poems such as "Common Folks Become Murderous, and "Trapped in an Ocean of Red Slogans."

Later, the Red Guards took away all Chen Yinke's medications from abroad and started actual beatings. Later still, they forced Chen and his wife out of their home into a hovel, where their daughters could visit only infrequently and at great political risk. The daughters were also pressured to denounce their father in public. By 1967, Chen Yinke had no illusions about the fact that the Red Guards aimed to kill him. His greatest grief was for his hard-suffering partner, Tang Yun. His last recorded verses (rendered here as "Funeral Oration for My Wife Before She Leaves") were addressed to her.

Finally, death came in the cruelest way imaginable. A man who had craved only a bit of solitude and some light, was imprisoned in a claustrophobic chamber with blaring loudspeakers right outside his window. The Red Guards assigned to "re-educate" Chen Yinke knew that the blind cripple was also an insomniac. So they moved the loudspeakers right next to Chen Yinke's bed and turned up the volume even louder. He died on the 7th of October 1969, literally crushed by the noise and the lies broadcasted about all that he had once held dear. His wife, refusing her medications, died less than two months later.[12]

Although Chen's death could not have been more inhuman, his life bears witness to the resilience of a deeply cultured humanity. As I read through the corpus of Chen Yinke's poetry, this subtle source of enduring strength became increasingly apparent. It was not only the grace of words in many occasional jottings that was impressive; it was also the intensity of his attachment to language itself. Beyond the forest of allusions, so helpfully decoded by Chinese researchers such as Yu Yingshi and Hu Wenhui, I glimpsed a faith in what I have termed "ancestral intelligence."[13] This is an idea that radiates out of the old form of the character *ling*, which combines the meanings of "brilliant," "creative" and "adept at adapting."

Building upon this one word, I look back at Chen Yinke's life, and it seems considerably less bleak than the chronology of sufferings and blackened photographs might convey. Blind and crippled, Chen remained a spirited man; or rather, a man with a spritely soul. It is that agility that I have tried to recover in poems about the impoverishment of speech (and thought) in Mao's China.

"If Chinese Characters are not Destroyed, China Will Die"

The war on language in 20th Century China did not start with Mao Zedong. It had been a passionate cause among radical intellectuals from the 1910s onward. China's foremost writer, Lu Xun (1881-1936), a reluctant experimenter with vernacular speech himself, said this in the heat of the New Culture Movement: "If Chinese characters are not destroyed, China will die."[14] Fu Sinian (1896-1950), a young activist, also attacked traditional logographs. A decade before Fu became an eminent historian and a close friend of Chen Yinke, he had criticized classical language as the paltry scratchings of "ox demons" and "snake spirits" clawing their way out of a deadly hell.[15] With one hasty thrust, it would seem, the cultural revolutionaries of the 1910s were ready to cast all of Confucian culture onto the bonfire of vanities.

How could they have even imagined, in their worst nightmares, that the same phrases that they had used to condemn classical Chinese orthography and literature would come back to haunt their fellow scholars in the violent era of the Red Guards? Fu Sinian, who ended his career as Director of the Academia Sinica in Taiwan, had no way of knowing that "ox demons" and "snake spirits"—*niu gui she shen*—would be precisely the linguistic formula used to imprison and beat intellectuals to death in the 1960s. It is as if the past, misunderstood and maligned, rose up to consume the very elite once mandated to carry supple poetics forward into modern times.

The language revolutionaries of the 1910s had hoped that by abandoning Chinese characters, they could promote rapid literacy among the commoners. Romanized syllables and Esperanto held an endless fascination for men and women who nonetheless continued to write poems, love letters and short stories in the same old evocative characters that had been sacred for their grandparents. The final blow that ended their debates about vernacular speech and the legacy of the ancients came shortly after the Communist victory of 1949.

Mao Zedong, even before assuming total power, had been in favor of retaining some form of Chinese writing. Encouraged by Stalin to dress up the revolution with a "Chinese" face, Mao ordered the language authorities to start simplifying characters in the early 1950s. The first list of legally denuded characters was promulgated in January, 1956. In the 1960s, further party edicts augmented the pressure and the list. By the 21st Century, most Chinese on the mainland made do with a language so desiccated that it could be recognized by anyone "walking thru the Kwik-mart 2 by sumthing."[16]

This latter day impoverishment of speech is captured with empathy and insight by Peter Hessler in his book entitled *Oracle Bones*. Like Hessler, I do not see the grievous loss of nuanced speech on the Chinese mainland as merely China's tragedy. It mirrors a broader human impoverishment. As I worked my way through the writings of Chen Yinke, the forgotten sonorities of many languages rang through my ear and my heart. This may be because I grew up with a cacophony of words under Communism in Transylvania. At home we spoke Hungarian, and at school we studied Romanian, Russian and French. My parents spoke German to each other and Yiddish to my grandmother; they also hired a Hebrew tutor to teach me the basic vocabulary of Jewish tradition. Each of these languages had been threatened with various forms of diminishment and came to color the poems crafted for this volume.

Later, as I explored the Second Century etymological classic *Shuo Wen Jie Zi*, I discovered many connotations preserved in archaic Chinese characters. I excavated them in verses dedicated to single logographs in order to evoke for Western readers the generativity of tradition as a whole. Chen Yinke, of course, was familiar with all the meanings and nuances of the ancients' tongue. His manuscripts show a determination to use traditional, unsimplified ideograms long after the Communist regime had declared them illegal.

In 1929, when he eulogized his mentor, Wang Guowei, upon a public memorial, Chen made sure that the characters used reflected the beauty and the amplitude of meaning contained in the classical Chinese language. The top third of the black marble (that still graces the campus of Qinghua University today) was carved with the most ancient forms in order to reflect the freshest grief. Below them, in smaller script appears Chen's eloquent, lengthy tribute to Wang's scholarship and devotion to truth.

After Chen's own tragic death in 1969, his students and disciples obtained permission to carve a memorial stone and place it in a small garden off the beaten path on Lushan Mountain. With Mao and his cohorts almost forgotten by the late 1990s, Chen could be memorialized with some of the same words that he had used in praise of Wang Guowei. Out of the hundreds of complex characters Chen Yinke had penned in 1929, only ten are inscribed in flowing

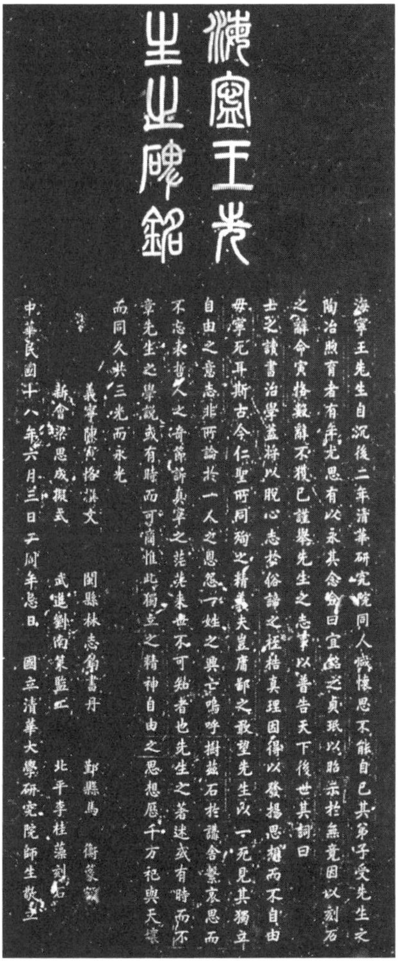

海寧王先生之碑銘

海寧王先生自沉後二年清華研究院同人咸懷思不能自已其弟子受先生之陶冶煦育者有年尤思有以永其念僉曰宜銘之貞珉以昭示於無竟因以刻石之辭命寅恪數辭不獲已謹舉先生之志事以普告天下後世其詞曰士之讀書治學蓋將以脫心志於俗諦之桎梏真理因得以發揚思想而不自由毋寧死耳斯古今仁聖所同殉之精義夫豈庸鄙之敢望先生以一死見其獨立自由之意志非所論於一人之恩怨一姓之興亡嗚呼樹茲石於講舍繫哀思而不忘表哲人之奇節訴真宰之茫茫來世不可知者也先生之著述或有時而不章先生之學說或有時而可商惟此獨立之精神自由之思想歷千萬祀與天壤而同久共三光而永光

義寧陳寅恪撰文　閩縣林志鈞書丹　鄞縣馬衡篆額

新會梁思成擬式　武進劉南策監工　北平李桂藻刻石

中華民國十八年六月三日二周年忌日　國立清華大學研究院師生敬立

green ink upon a simple rock. These contain a slogan for a new generation of intellectuals longing for qualities of mind still proscribed by the Communist regime: “Independence of Spirit, Freedom of Thought”—*duli zhi jingshen, ziyou zhi sixiang.*

These two memorial stones converse with and interrogate each other. The fullness of expression permitted during the 1920s—even when the subject was as grim as Wang’s suicide and widespread political corruption—shrank during subsequent decades. The small number of Chinese words on the mountain stone convey a more easily digested message: *Try to be like Chen Yinke in spirit and thought; and if that is not possible, let your mind’s eye graze a few calligraphic images about his life with unabashed envy.* Interestingly, the ten characters used on Chen’s memorial stone have not been simplified by the Communist regime. They express what needs saying in the cadence of the ancients, invigorated by a modern brush.

My own poems in this volume strive

for a similar alchemy. With this ambition, I stand in a long line of Western writers who have drawn fresh inspiration from logographs and Chinese poets. As I was penning my own works, I kept wondering what Chen Yinke might have said if he could have met contemporaries such as Ernest Fenollosa or Ezra Pound at Harvard, in Berlin or in Kyoto. Would Chen have been heartened by foreigners who looked to Chinese characters for inspiration in crafting a new poetic idiom? I suspect he would have been amused by some of Fenollosa's conjectures about exotic logographs and his plan for their "fructification" in English-language poetry.[17] Perhaps if he had read Pound's *Confucian Odes*, Chen might have been delighted by a literary harvest denied to his own countrymen by the exigencies of war and revolution.

In Chen Yinke's life there was very little sanction for a slow-paced exploration of thought and speech, something that Western poets are able to achieve rather readily today. To be sure, the shadow of historical trauma in the 20th Century stretched far beyond China's borders. Nonetheless, the might of language authorities has been more limited abroad than in Beijing or in Canton. Therefore, it is a bit easier to act upon Hannah Arendt's injunction to enlist language in the service of humanity.

I am not the pariah that Chen Yinke became during the reign of Mao Zedong. I lack the tools of his monumental scholarship concerning classical Chinese literature and history. But I can listen. I can bend my ear toward a time of darkness that nonetheless carried a thread of light. That thread ties together the poems of this volume. They reflect how conscience and vision survived at the very heart of the language. In this molten core, I understand what W.H. Auden meant when he wrote, "Words have no word for words that are not true."[18]

Ancestral Intelligence

Part I

傷

Words Have No Word

Renditions after Chen Yinke

Midnight Sun (1911)

I cast my loneliness
on northern seas,
seek out words
silenced
by borderless
immensities.

On this voyage north,
and still father north,
where earth's girdle
is loosened by diminishing
latitudes, heaven
is battered
by gulls, puffins, albatross
heading south.

Here, slanted rays guard a giant
moon, and for one moment,
I hear fresh verses from my old land,
its laughter a rhyming chant.

Suddenly, I dream of bamboo,
Yellow River's fishing junks,
guests crowding my courtyard,

far, far from Norway's
chilling midnight sun.

Ibsen's Grave (1911)

After ten days' journey, solace
in a frost-embroidered land,

a few distant stars
and a long night's moon
deepen the delight
of lacquered snow,
sapphire seas.

I come here to mourn
and bless you, Ibsen.

Your northern rhymes
freed the tongue
of literary arts.

When will you also rouse
our eastern shores
from somnolence?

Your plain talk,
astounding mirth
pound in my ears
like the hammer on your tomb,

fearless
and solitary.

Exile's Hope (1919)

We become one man
awash in dreams
as you tell old stories
from back home.

The sting of recollection
rouses new hope:
maybe here,
in exile,
we will craft
even livelier tales,

brimming with wonder,
illumined by electric bulbs,
mirroring the sheen
of ancient cinnabar.

This night's prattle
meanders along a foreign river,
revives a sorrowful soul

as if no earthly shadows followed.

Ripples in American Waters (1919)

At the Paris Peace Conference,
they are toying
with the future
of our country.

Here, along the lake
at Wellesley College,
we mutter about love,
and war.

In the shade of bending willows
dappled by the morning sun,
we ask each other:

Can guests in the house
of foreign tongues,
ever mourn
native wrongs?

Suddenly,
red brick colonials
lose their charm,
artfully crafted
window boxes
grow less verdant

as we turn to embrace
this autumn's grief.

The Culture of Our Divine Land (1927)

All that made our culture
divine

lies buried
with you.

How dare I mourn
as if it were
my sorrow
alone?

Sir, you wept
when no righteous army
came to the rescue
of our despoiled land;
when ancestors called
your name
to bear their shame
bone
deep.

The chatter of academics
churned around you;
their jealousy
left no room
for a life
of truth.

Weary, you chose death
though your scholar's brush
remained a fit companion
for Heaven's Will.

The lofty lake that took your body
must now endure
the endless whimper
of odious crows.

Carved in Black Alabaster (1929)

Can mere stone mirror
a philosopher's calling?

Two years after you drowned
yourself, Sir, the tranquil seas
trailing your youth
still roil with grief.

Those who knew you and shared
the hard labor of scholarship,
are now burdened by the salt
of longing and regret.

No lasting memorial
has yet been carved;
nothing but black
alabaster will do.

Can mere stone speak
the language of integrity?

They sought me out for words
suitable for engraving,
but dawn after dawn
I push off their request.

It finds me again,
speaking the tongue
of future generations.

How, then, to describe
a soul's ambition?

All you hoped was to refine
the brush of learning,
cut the chains
of vulgarity
so truth
might
soar.

You did not drown yourself
to settle a private peeve
or protest politics of the hour:

Where thought could not be free,
death was a more welcome companion.

This is not the *dao*
of mediocre men.

Only sages are willing martyrs
for mind's unfettered reach.

Time will come
when your writings
will shed no light,
when no one
will recall
your name,
your books.

Even in that hellish night, Sir,
your lonely soul
and fierce heart

will illuminate ten thousand pages,
more than the sun and moon together.

Worse than Murderous Old Women (1930)

Once an arrow is drawn inside the bow
there is no stopping,

nor can this pen
cease painting
men like mindless oxen
shoving under the windows
of the powerful, pretending
their bellows
call for freedom.

Learned men are useless
when jesters strike a pose
for the biographer's brush.

Too much ink already wasted on China's tales
of bawdy bandits and murderous old women.

Why bother croaking against comrades
who confound the truth?

Disjointed Times (1937)

Aimlessly, I go to greet
a barbarous spring,
seek out a lake
where I mourn
alone.

What is the use of reading history
only to have premonitions of fading
flowers, recall men who are
no more?

No one remembers an old monk
who would rather starve
than have nothing new
to teach.

These are disjointed times:
pomegranates bloom
blood red,
pagoda trees
predictably
jade green,

while the broken bones of our country
lie scattered and a cold, cold
wind sweeps autumn's gloom
into the guesthouse.

Bitter rains beat down remaining blossoms,
noisy sparrows chatter as crowds stumble into chaos,

beggars pick through the baggage of exile.

I wring my hands,
bemoan the Will of Heaven,
wait for the deadly fight to start,
for my hair to turn white.

After the War (1945)

Distant bells bring thin hope
as crows take refuge
in forest shadows.

My life is marred
by premonitions:

there is no hero
to face a fading sun
while our shattered land
grabs victory's spoils,
heedless

of the long chill coming.

The season of open gates
and bashful honeysuckle
has vanished.

I pretend
this is my old home.

To My Wife (1946)

Dreams pursue me on this ship
heading home, England a vanishing
hope, Panama the narrow straits
toward our land
threadbare from war.

In one nightmare,
an ancient courtier cries out:
This body not yet dead
is fit for worms alone.

I reach for our silken marriage quilt
and wake to the coarse burlap
of our separation,
the lead weight
of this cursed blindness.

Distance has tattered my words;
pennies we once saved
have all been sunk
into old books.

There is no ballast
for this barge trembling
on yellow seas.

No One to Rescue Words (1946)

Turning fifty-six is more painful
than being cut in pieces.

My ailing eyes
are dead.

They still call me a man,
but I am a ghost,
even as our home
fills with birthday laughter.

In the alley next door,
they are freshening an altar
for a long-forgotten ancestor.

Specters and poets
share the same grief:

thousands of old books
gnawed by sighing worms
call out to us,

yet we have no power
to rescue fallen words.

History's chronicles,
the ancients' verses
drift off the page
into oblivion,
a slimy trail
where I once heard
the breath of life.

Unbearably Verdant (1947)

Spring spills over our ancient capital
as I arrive broken
to a vanished world,
find no vessel
to contain
a mourner's tears.

Flowering peach in country courtyards
are not the ones
I cherished
twenty years ago,
yet each gate proclaims:
You rested here,
you tasted an afternoon's
fragrant tea.

A cruel dream.

Alien envoys now take
their troublesome ease
in our lofty towers,
while ruined temples
harbor a few
wizened scholars.

Alone,
I cradle worries like jewels
for an emperor cursed
to defend palaces
flattened by war.

On the Boulevard of Eternal Peace
youth roam with barbarian hearts.

Hurried Out of the City of Northern Peace (1948)

On the fifteenth day of the twelfth month
in the foreigners' calendar,
Red armies near the capital,

heavenly signs askew.

At the gate of a gutted garden,
I step into a car, rush to the airfield,
send this to you, dear friend—

three times already
we have endured chaos, separations;
now, even the sages' tears
cannot convey our grief.

I look back
on beloved streets and alleys,
dreams of coming back north
abandoned.

What use is one letter
in a world turned
upside down?

I know
our country's tragedy
is greater
than this hurried,
hurried parting.

Warning (1949)

Today, an azure bird brings word
from the Queen Mother of the West,
a thousand jade-brushed seeds,
one warning:

My people, how can you grovel so?

Are you no more than an aged whore
weeping at autumn's gate,
mourning the breeze
that fails to pry it open?

Where are your dreams?

What do you say to ancients
who risked everything
for one noble deed?

Don't you see
tomorrow's ashes?

On the Seventh Day of the Seventh Lunar Month (1949)

This is the time the Milky Way promised
to bridge all parted lovers,

yet from our curtained bed
we hear another prophecy:

seasons are shifting
with a biting chill;

quivering shadows have fallen
over mountain laurel;

wild winds wake
rising tides;

the golden vessel
of our motherland

lies tarnished, shrunken
like a waning moon.

To part now
would agonize the soul

endlessly. How to swallow
longing for joys we shared,

fight off the dread of months
lying in wait?

Bombing (1950)

Orange lanterns once heralded
the start of a new year.

Now, weather worries
golden mimosa into bloom
on a day snows should fall.

This day,
hundreds of corpses
drift on Canton River,
each a rudderless barge.

Where men once lived,
crazed dogs, emaciated oxen,
motherless fowl
litter the streets,
rotting prawn, the shore.

The stench of fear reigns
unchallenged in our city.

No moon goddess can heal
this much grief.

Dreams (1951)

All night I travel
water highways rushing
past marble pavilions,
terraced gardens,
lacquered temple gates.

Why bother to brush
another verse
about the lonely lilac?

Afterlife (1953)

Stalin's dead and the rattle
of Korea's ending war
echoes through our jade paradise.

The Party's crimson palaces bulge,
bloated with slogans
from clever leaders.

New immortals,
they drink themselves into oblivion,
squelch rumors like poisonous weeds.

A sober man
must look beyond
the haze,

reflect on past events
even as rulers chant:
The afterlife is here on earth.

Many would mock my wish
to grab at distant galaxies,
clutch a handful of their dust
to fashion a durable armor,

some weapon
against the mawkish prattle
heard on the streets today.

Blind Man's Cane (1954)

Fifteen years ago, a friend
gave me a yellow maple walking stick;
he took the trouble to have it inscribed
like scrolls of old:
a rod to rectify all evils.

Now, it has become a faithful
companion, loosening our grip at night,
firming the bond at dawn again;
weak, I bend into its strength,
a supple dragon reminding me to stand firm.

As our nation's calamities
grow numberless,
I learn to cherish
stubborn knots,
rough edges,
peeling bark.

Though blind, I look for pebbled paths,
my cane a mentor in Heaven's ways,
keeping me from the broad avenues

peopled by smooth talkers
spicing up dishes for the palate
of the powerful.

Heroes (1955)

Ruthless seas have shredded
history's grand design,

while I forage black forests
for any trace of heroes.

From ancients to the present,
how many dared to desire

the end of hatred?
This chronicle of names

is not long enough
for a single night's

vanishing
dream.

Poems Enough for My Beheading (1956)

Red clouds shadow
my 66th birthday
as I call to mind
a jade-green sea,
storied pavilions.

Eight scorching years
in this place.

Like a simple weaver woman
who plies her trade to feed
a husband starved
by politics and exile,

my wife still strives
to put long-eared mushrooms
before us.

Her hard labors should have
earned her titles of nobility,

not this life
where all my books
add bricks to our tomb.

These evening years
are filled with poems
enough for my beheading,

and convivial laughter
with wine of winter plum.

Cawing (1957)

Ah, the ancients' long-drained passion
for delicate jades and tender teas,
their plays of reverie and doomed love,
shatter my seclusion—

one shard of an aria
brings them all back.

I travel less these days as winds
grow fierce; year upon year
diminishes me.

A gentle drizzle suddenly wakes
crested starlings,
as if these were auspicious times.

In my old garden, newly loosed
peony petals blanket the ground
where southern kingdoms
swallowed one another,
heedlessly.

I don't believe
today's Immortals
with their chants
of blossoming
freedom.

They are pure talk.
They have no plans

for monkhood.

Better to hum Tang melodies,
let a smile brush my lips,
the capital's cawing
drowned by autumn dreams.

Old Knots (1957)

Bamboo grows more sinewy
beneath western winds,

which also polish the winter pear,
spread news of greening onions,
purpling plum.

Such supple growth
recalls the cultured charms
of ancient rulers who knew
how to bend into adversity.

As long as spring winds blow
and bamboo knots grow tougher,
no one needs to teach me
the art of shouldering
a year's heavy months.

Rush-Leaf Swords (1957)

This year's new fashion requires
much tailoring, trimming,
as waves from Hunan
ruffle our robes.

Spring plums rain upon the lute,
waking her complaint;
gusts of lotus-scented wind
harry a smooth brow.

In villages and in the ruler's palace
old folks play at pulling
puppet strings, as ocean's bounty
piles prawns in bamboo baskets.

Better stay drunk, savor one autumn's
pomegranate bloom,
than this bitter teaching:
rush-leaf swords

are powerless against the clang
of iron chains.

Mourning for Language and Land (1962)

On bound feet, sporting a scholar's robe,
the Ming courtesan Liu Rushi
crosses the river, a fateful visit
in strange clothes; now man for a day,
beloved bride for years.

Decades later, her writing brush
inks grief on winter willow
when China is swallowed
by barbarian rulers.

The learned ways of ancient daughters
teach Liu how to watch for snow
like catkins in the wind.

Before he is jailed in early spring,
her husband still paints her eyebrows
lovingly, content to be no more
than trampled grass
on eastern mountains.

No need to seek office from conquerors—
one fragrant blossom consoles his aged heart.

Lovers of shadows, these two
are harshly silenced:

the Master of Crimson Clouds
is taken prisoner first;

in a few months,
Liu who sought refuge
in the Tower of Listening for Truth
cuts her own throat—

no one is left to share her mourning
for him, for language, and for land.

A Chilling Spring (1963)

Cranes know this year
is as cold as when
the wise emperor died.

Illness rides this carriage
rattling back home in a chilling spring
as gloom glowers through ceaseless rain.

How dare a man
with wasting body
long for the glory of a thousand autumns?

Even my own years I cannot count,
leaving such matters in expert hands
which pen the chronicle of my ailments.

Last year, at this time,
my spirit already kept company
with wintry winds;

they chased away the cranes,
leaving me to sigh for a world
once peopled by unicorns.

Divination (1963)

Today I name myself
a man whose time
has passed, whose body
will end on a desolate
rattan mat—

this divination
comes unbidden,
like a crow's caw
long after sunset.

Southern gardens once blessed
by a bountiful heaven
shiver as north winds howl
on this New Year's day.

I've shuttered the gate
against noble well-wishers,
their sneering and rage
familiar.

Solitary Stalk (1964)

How deep the kinship of ancient historians
with China's dreamers!

Both wove garlands of humble flowers
out of the words princes had shunned.

Today, when ruination reigns,
pity the hollyhock

blooming
alone.

Skull of Mercy (1964)

I have heard from afar
that in the land of Western bamboo,
the shattered skull of Buddha's mercy
has found a resting place,

while here,
in China,

monumental regrets have imprisoned
my garrulous tongue,

no ink left to restore the ancients' scroll,
no silk threads to stitch one painful word
next to the other.

One Gaunt Brush (1964)

One day your poem, grandfather,
accosts me on a silken scroll.

We two share grief
while vain men

crowd the pages
of our history.

Startled into loss
and understanding,

I lift
one gaunt brush,

satiate the horse hairs
with tears of lead,

paint mulberry fields
swallowed by the blackest sea.

History's Rubble (1964)

This they call
being human!

Condemned already
a thousand times,
my crime?
I write.

When I can steal an hour
from shouting crowds,
I seek solace in poems
by a courtesan who killed
herself when dynasties
collapsed, when heaven
and earth traded light,
leaving unspeakable darkness.

I'd climb divine heights
to gaze on history's rubble, find
a sheltering mountain, gentle
leave-taking from worldly cares,
the voice within the silence.

Peony Market (1965)

Even if every shred
of our tradition
be cannibalized,
every old man
become a torn book,
every bronze tripod
left to tarnish in the trash,
condemned,

the peony market goes on,
one flower hawker singing
Tang arias in praise
of the filmiest yellows,
another shouting the names
of Han heroes who died
for the brashest rose.

I go home to take refuge
in the lonely charm
of winter plum,

knowing
that mighty ghosts
outside the market gate
have lost the art of worshiping
the King of Flowers.

Common Folk Become Murderous (1966)

Common folk have become
murderous in the wounded
presence of the great.

Like rouged harlots,
they plot darkly how to weed
out truth; like the monkey king
they stuff hovels with rotting fruit.

Songs of the hour mimic compassion
while I hear the howl
of slavering hounds.

Could these be the descendants
of ancestors who practiced
the art of modest dreams?

Long ago, I might have scaled
mountains for ink
to tell their tales.

Today, I look back
on thirty years, a deadly
end in sight,

my soul's shore
littered with withering fish.

The Day I Should Have Swept Family Graves (1967)

What use this ashen morning
to climb ancestral tombs,
burn paper money to ease
the troubles of the dead,
dwell in dreams
ferrying me to father's grave?

Fiery Mars heralds this new year,
hastened by a desire to burn history.

My own soul shatters
on coarse cement
beneath the feet
of a maddened crowd
in the distant south.

Here, my beloved wife
lies weak from illness;
our wary daughters
walk by slowly, silent.

I recall the Cold Food Festival,
when we still honored the sage
who chose to perish
rather than serve a craven lord.

Ocean of Red Slogans (1967)

Sparrows clamor between the eaves,
reporting an early spring.
Last night, northern winds
ripped through the outer gate.

This morning, I tried to pretend
I am man at peace.

A shrunken face,
maimed eyes
mock the flimsy fable.

Disasters hang heavy
on this rice-begging body;
ghost stories swell
as Crimson City
fires up for idol worship.

In these warring times,
every talisman
against evil
has lost its luster.

Funeral Oration for My Wife, Before She Leaves (1968)

I bury my face in a fetid
burlap blanket fit for cattle,
like the impoverished scholar
from the Han.

His shivering nightmares
were auguries of hope
compared to the bitter rains
drenching our hovel.

His wife's tears became a shield
for virtue, until the day a ruler
rose who knew the worth
of learned men,

while I, a maimed
and useless remnant
cannot hide you from calamity.

I only plead—
linger a little longer
by hell's nine rivers.

This man with withered eyes
will follow.

Same Dream, Same Mirror (1945-1960)

We have dreamt the same dream
during many unraveling autumns;
one joy, one worry binds us.

Sweet or bitter, we mark
each fall, no longer haunted
by grief or rancor.

We put on faces
before the same mirror;
our small flight of swallows
is secure. We hear
immortal music
on ancient bronze bells.

The hills and valleys of our sorrows
map many pages as we laugh
before night's lantern, never tire
of the ancients' brush and sword,
hide ourselves in dense mountains,
become immortal.

Knifing winds arrive
to pierce this body.
A single rattan couch
holds all our sorrows
as one more spring
startles illness
into exhaustion.

Green shadows gather a curtain
to shield us as we listen
for the cicada's cry.

Rehearsing our years,
we find solace
in yielding seasons.

Even when bitter rains
leave us desolate,
one summer evening's chatter
is enough—
cicadas sing.

Part II

Words that Are Not True

Logograph Poems by Vera Schwarcz

“Abundance”

Life sank roots
deep into the loam
of calligraphy
as

feng

豐

garnished with leafy boughs
made room for an altar
where gratitude might sprout.

The giving heart, despoiled,
bequeathed

feng

丰

three
naked
latitudes

pierced by a sharp nail
to pin down
what once ached
upward.

"Aging"

The old Chinese
logograph

sui

歲

could not be rushed:
Limbs of dwarf-pine,
a summit of stillness,
made getting old
into a lustrous journey,
a melody drawn out of fluted,
frayed bamboo.

Today's

sui

岁

slammed
a mountain
onto a tottering
sickle moon.

Aging—
a tired body,
tilts
toward
senility,

no longer an art
of the carefully
cultivated heart-mind.

"Ancestral Intelligence"

Fairies and elves once kept vigil
at ancestral graves, dancing shamans
prayed for rain.

Ling

靈

rippled with nimble feet,
while heirs harvested
a quickening mind.

When
moderns
let
go
of
rain
and
rhyme
and prayer,

ling

灵

lingered as a claw
over quivering flames.

"Birth"

Language was once
a capacious womb.
When birth became a slogan,
fecundity, like reason,
shrank.

Chan

產

which once was
a child rippling,
wiggling out
of a wrinkled
birth canal,
alive,
is gutted,
these days.

No infant
cries,
only
the whirr
of production.

Chan

产

forgets
deliverance,
masters the talk
of property and power.

"Burning"

Ancients venerated
earthly flames—

shao

燒

stacked kettles of savory stew
upon the hearth to honor
guests who cherished
a feast of classics,
not just fatty meat.

Later,

shao

烧

was stoked
with swords,
not food
for the spirit.

"Business"

Daily affairs were once painted
with a verdant canopy—

ye

業

a man crowned
by worthy deeds
calling to Heaven
in every
worker's
tongue.

Later,

ye

叶

starved
by
commerce,
coiled itself into a karmic curse,

no foliage to shelter men
with broken spines.

"Chaos"

Even confusion
had its sonorities
when

luan

亂

was drawn with a skilled hand
unraveling silk threads upward,
against the grain.

Politics
dragged
chaos
into
a dark
cave,

luan

乱

a sharp
tongue
cursing,
a primal
rebellion.

"Companions"

Lush cornfields swayed
companionably,
a multitude
of men at peace
before

chai

儕

was mowed
down,
decapitated.

A singular
man
tries
to
hold
up

chai

侪

while his culture
totters, drunk
on deracinated harmonies.

"Compassion"

Pity was once a brimming heart
when

lian

seasoned with rice wine
and nights of lute solos
was still a passionate echo
between the living
and the dead.

Now,

lian

怜

barks
a curt
command
glued
to daylight's
fragile backbone:

Be compassionate!

Shards of ancestral attachments
are silenced,
along with the unappeased ghosts
of nightime grief.

"Corporeality"

Bodies once built
firmly upon bones
stood as sacred
vessels,

ti

體

corporeality as an amplitude
stitched together with
sinew and song.

When

ti

体

took
shape
as
one
man
rooted
to no soil,

the tangible and the real
broke their bond,
mind's marrow
gutted.
Touch, a blind seer,
went groping for a useless cane.

“Courage”

When moderns could no longer
paint flesh on sinews
of speech,

dan

膽

raised its voice;
bravery became
a red dawn
braying.

Dan

胆

was nothing
but raw sun,
brawn
and
audacity,

not modest valor
behind veiled words.

"Desire"

was once unabashedly mutual.

Xing

drew forth desire
with two hands,
a joyful arching upward
toward the pedestal of elation—

until simplifying authorities
decreed: erase the hands,
let

xing

兴

lie
with three chicken scratches
upon the heart's despoiled altar.

"Dreams"

Night was a sheltering continent
where sages dreamt with squinted eyes
while

meng

夢

meandered a myriad
heavenly kingdoms.

These days

meng

梦

leaves restless
dreamers
only an
earthly destination:

a forest
weighing down
a fragile moon.

"Embrace"

had lowered eyes
when ancient Chinese held
each other closely.

Huai

懷

enveloped the heart
with a roof and a robe
ample enough
for lowered eyelids,
hidden affections.

Lately, a rough unveiling:
"embrace" has become
haggard

huai

怀

a naked body
leaning on a tattered soul.

"Flight"

Before airplanes and swiftly
sailing junks, ancients
took time to picture
flight as

fei

one crane aloft
glimpsed from below:
wondrous wings wide,
each quill a poem.

Dequilled,

fei

飞

hangs
in the air,
a breathless
frog,
a sail fin
drying
on Gobi
sands.

"Harmony"

Back when oracle bones
were inscribed with a generous knife,
pleasure, music, laughter
were all one picture—

yue

樂

chimed between two bells,
a drum poised delicately
on an altar, ancestors audible
in their rejoicing as descendents
vivified forgotten harmonies.

Now,

yue

乐

slashed
by six
brief
strokes,
pictures
joy
as a scrawny tree
beneath a broken roof,

slim consolation
for rulers and commoners alike.

"Homecoming"

The arc of return
had sturdy feet
in ancient China,

gui

歸

built up with brawn
and longing, like a boy
dreaming the bride
of his youth.

All that remains
these days of

gui

归

is a homely
broom,
mud
tracks
in a ravaged courtyard,

thistles blooming
among shards of clay.

"Idling"

The art of listening
is no longer a Chinese pastime
since the Party
shrank language,
calling it simplified.

Xian

was once a word picture
sages sang out with joy:

the idea of *idle* sheltered by two gates,
a gibbous moon risen between them,

the art of listening to heaven
refined by lingering
at the door posts of the unsaid,
alert to what steals
in and out of language at ease.

Xian

闲

is a poor cousin today
to the idleness of yore:

a broken
arch,

one
solitary
tree,

a boney finger
wagging at anyone who dares
moan where ruination grows.

One word,
diminished,
leaves a nation mute.

"Maimed"

Even a broken man,
sheltered,
savored hope
when

fei

廢

showed
how the injured
could yet be whole
in spirit.

In the new age
when the useless is discarded

fei

废

pictures
a badgered
body disrobed,

labels the lame and homeless
throw-aways.

"Maps"

Tu

圖

was once
three fields guiding a traveler
across borders, each pointing a path
for those willing to wander.

Today,
a shrunken
heart
has
barricaded
itself
inside

tu

图

Gone the grassy guides,
gone the license to stray
from field to field.

Instead, a frigid warning:
Stay out, winter reigns
unchallenged here.

"No Hurry"

On oracle bones, ancient rhinos
ambled slowly, circumambulating,
never on time in

chi

with its watery amplitude,
plenty of room for fairies
and unhurried reverence.

Later,

chi

迟

became
fleet
of foot,

no bovine
tardiness
allowed,
no
lingering
along
angels'
shores,

not even a hasty bow
to old Confucius.

"Painting"

Landscapes, colophons, poems
once ran with music of a single
horse-tail brush—

hua

畫

glistened with black ink
and the thirst of fine rice paper.

Arid
now,

hua

画

sinks
into
soil
like
an iron
plow,

deaf to the harmonies
of the scholar's brush
flowing like wind-blown grass.

"Recognition"

Telling one mountain from another
was once a sonorous journey,

shi

識

doubling vistas and vision,
guiding the lance of knowledge
until it landed softly in the loam of wisdom.

Later, when mountains thinned
like gruel for the poor,

shi

识

grew a wintery carapace,
a field of dead twigs
to narrow the panorama
of the eyes, make them forget
lacebark pine and brittle mosses.

"Sound"

The ear was once essential
for tasting sound as

sheng

聲

rippled through stone chimes,
strung on silken ropes;
mallet in hand,
ringers awakened music
in listening minds.

Without
mallet
or
chimes,
the ear
withered.

Tone-deaf
ghosts
howl
these
days
while

sheng

声

is mute—a black void.

"Startled"

The soul aroused
used be carried aloft
on horseback
when

jing

驚

awakened sleep-thick brows
and a cacophony of hoof beats
still troubled the slumber
of corrupt officials.

Later,
when men's naked hearts,
took up residence
in a trembling city,

jing

惊

without the beat
of hooves
troubled
no one's
sleep,
itself a sheep

for hungry wolves.

"Tears"

A dog used to lurk
near heart's gate,
when

lei

rippled with velvet shame
and a man's wet face stretched
upon the canvass of grief
still carried traces
of the calligrapher's brush.

When
eyes
became
mere
eyes,
water
just
water,

lei

泪

left no trace of humanity
to weep reluctant rivulets
into China's grief-seasoned seas.

"Temple"

An edifice once roomy enough
for emperor, priest and peasant,

miao

廟

used to sift dross from prayers,
incense clouds enveloping the hopeful
whether they called on Laotzu, Confucius,
Buddha or his servant, the Dalai Lama.

Later
they
gutted

miao

庙

leaving a single gable
to shelter guardians
of China's dried up wells.

Appeals to Heaven once painted
with fifteen breaths of the brush,
are chocked now by a few scrawny strokes.

"Temple"
sounds the same,
but greets the eye
like a profane scar.

"Timeless"

Olden days were graced
with feathered owls
and the mortar of classics,
as

jiu

舊

was conjured up
afresh each day,
ink stone ready
and a scholar's brush
giving the past its wings.

In the new republic
of the masses,
nocturnal birds
migrate to Tibet,
while

jiu

旧

lingers,
a ragged
reminder
of banished fowl and beast.

Only one downward
slash
stands by scorched shadows
on parched pavement.

"Tranquility"

Peace of mind once rippled
in a bowl of rice wine
making no waves at all,
an imperceptible nod
toward sea and silk
when

ning

寧

claimed dominion
over heart and mind alike.

Later,
they
nailed

ning

宁

to
an
iron
wall.

Silk, too, unraveled,
revealing a shabby prison
for unquiet words.

"Wound"

What is injury
without an arrow?
Warriors used to guard
their armor when

shang

傷

tinted hurt
with a cloud-piercing sun.

Today's brushwork
leaves

shang

伤

lonely
alongside
power,
a wound
of the spirit,

a raw ache
as if a bully has
slammed
a heavy seal
on thin rice paper.

“Writing”

Xie

写

crouches near
broken eaves
because winged
writing has lost her
melodious
slippers,

memories of a curvaceous lute
slashed by strings of industrial steel.

Still, you can hear the ancients’ brush,
painting and writing
with one breath:

xie.

NOTES: INTRODUCTION

1. Hannah Arendt, *Men in Dark Times* (New York, 1955).
2. Isabelle Revol, *Chen Yinke: un intellectuel au service de la liberté dans la Chine contemporaine* (Berlin, 2010) p. 33. This campaign is also discussed in Bian Senghui, *Chen Yinke xiansheng nianpu changbian* (a draft chronology of the life of Chen Yinke) (Beijing, 2010) pp. 306-310.
3. Wen-hsin Yeh, "Historian and Courtesan: Chen Yinke and the Writing of Liu Rushi Biezhuan," Morrison Lecture (July, 2003) p. 7.
4. For a further discussion of "Ibsenism" and Hu Shi in the New Culture Movement, see: Vera Schwarcz, *The Chinese Enlightenment: Intellectuals and the Legacy of the May Fourth Movement of 1919* (Berkeley, 1986) as well as Kwok-Kan Tam, *Ibsen in China 1908-1997* (Hong Kong, 2001).
5. The reaction of leftist intellectuals to the suicide of Wang Guowei is discussed in: Lawrence A. Schneider, *Ku Chieh-kang and China's New History* (Los Angeles, 1971) pp. 123-128.
6. I am indebted to my editor Rennie McQuilkin for suggesting this analogy between Chen Yinke and Tiresias in one of our early conversations about the blind historian-poet. The power of this analytical link became even more compelling in April, 2012, when I was giving a public lecture about Chen Yinke just as another blind dissident—Chen Guangcheng—crawled his way out of the clutches of local authorities in Shandong province. During the days that this latter-day Chen spent inside the U.S. Embassy in Beijing, the press contacted me repeatedly to speak about both men who were named Chen, both blind and both gazing more deeply into society's dark secrets than most of their contemporaries.
7. The original Chinese of this poetic fragment appears in Yue Nan, *Chen Yinke yu Fu Sinian* (Chen Yinke and Fu Sinian) (Xi'an, 2008) p. 319.
8. Chen Yinke's refusal to pursue required political study is discussed at length in the preface of Yu Yingshi, *Chen Yinke wannian shi zeng* (a corrective elucidation of the literary works produced by Chen Yinke in his later years), (Taibei, 1984).
9. Lu Jiandong, *Chen Yinke de zuihou ershi nian* (re the last twenty years of Chen Yinke's life) (Beijing, 1995).
10. A contemporary example of a painting about the virtue of *qijie* may be found in the work of Cantonese artist Li Dajun, who was drawn to windswept bamboo in an effort to comment, indirectly, on official corruption in China. This theme is discussed on Li's website, *http://ldjart.cn/blog/article.asp.?id=8.*

11. Wen-hsin Yeh, op. cit, p. 13.

12. Zhang Qiuhui, *Chen Yinke de jiazu shi* (the family history of Chen Yinke) (Guangzhou, 2000) p. 314.

13. My understanding of Chen Yinke's poetry has been greatly aided by the following two studies: Yu Yingshi, *Chen Yinke wannian shi wen shi zheng* (cited above) and Hu Wenhui, *Chen Yinke jian shi* (annotations on the poetry of Chen Yinke) (Guangzhou, 2008).

14. Yueh-ping Yen, *Calligraphy and Power in Contemporary China* (London, 2005) p. 105.

15. Ibid.

16. Peter Hessler, *Oracle Bones: A Journey Through Time in China* (New York, 2006), p. 417.

17. Ernest Fenollosa and Ezra Pound, *The Chinese Written Character as a Medium for Poetry* (London, 1920) p. 4.

18. W.H. Auden, "Words," in *Collected Poems* (New York, 1997) p. 93.

NOTES: PART I

MIDNIGHT SUN (1911). Ill with beriberi, Chen Yinke nonetheless took a difficult 10-day journey from Berlin to Norway, bent upon visiting Ibsen's grave.

IBSEN'S GRAVE (1911). When Chen Yinke finally arrived at Ibsen's grave, he was greatly impressed by the hauntingly white carving of a hammer on the memorial stone—a symbol of the will to awaken a slumbering population to fight against the lies that pass for repressive social mores. For Chen, the hammer also signaled the promise of a literary awakening.

EXILE'S HOPE (1919). This poem recalls the transformative encounter between Chen Yinke and the literary scholar Wu Mi (1894-1978), who was studying comparative literature at Harvard under Irving Babbitt. In Cambridge, Chen heard Wu lecture about China's 18th Century novel, *The Dream of the Red Chamber*—which became the subject of Wu's life-long scholarship. The two men remained friends and worked together to both preserve and enliven China's classical literary traditions.

RIPPLES IN AMERICAN WATERS (1919). During the Versailles Peace Conference of April-May, 1919 (while the Allies were deciding to hand over the Chinese province of Shandong to Japan), Chen Yinke spent some time visiting his friend Wu Maozu, who was engaged to a student at Wellesley College. The three young Chinese intellectuals engaged in endless debates about the fate of their motherland. They also bemoaned their own powerlessness at a time when their contemporaries in Beijing had launched a patriotic demonstration on May 4th, 1919.

THE CULTURE OF OUR DIVINE LAND (1927). In 1927, Chen Yinke's beloved mentor, Wang Guowei, committed suicide by drowning himself in Kunming Lake in the Summer Palace. At first, as this poem shows, Chen sunk into a deep depression that went beyond personal grief. It was as if all of China's land and waters were mourning a man who had sought to bring a measure of truth into a public life saturated by pettiness and lies. Two years later, Chen finally agreed to compose an official epitaph for Wang Guowei.

CARVED IN ALABASTER (1929). Throughout 1927 and 1928, Chen Yinke's colleagues at Qinghua University asked him to write an epitaph that would be worthy of being inscribed in stone. He repeatedly refused. Finally, very reluctantly, Chen agreed. As this rendition shows, he sensed that his own words, like Wang Guowei's scholarship, would have no enduring value in China's public life. In the short run, he was right. After the Cultural Revolution, however, both men's reputations have soared among Chinese intellectuals.

WORSE THAN MURDEROUS OLD WOMEN (1930). During the "Nanking Decade" (1927-1937) when the Nationalist Party of Jiang Kai-shek was in power, Chen did not become an open dissident. Instead, he chronicled his disenchantment with corrupt politicians and their academic "advisors" in bitter notes centered on traditional folk tales about female and male bandits.

DISJOINTED TIMES (1937). Chen Yinke's scholarship on the sinification of Buddhism began in 1933 with an essay on the 6th Century monk Zhi Mindu. Mindu had used the language of Chinese Daoism to argue for the non-existence of conscious thought. His clever adaptations in the service of a new Buddhist lexicon won him fame and followers—a situation which Mindu claimed he would gladly forsake if he had nothing new to teach.

AFTER THE WAR (1945). While most of his contemporaries celebrated the end of the war with Japan, an increasingly blind Chen Yinke became attuned to a deeper ravage that had destroyed old notions of "home" even before the Communists and the Nationalists took up arms against each other.

NO ONE TO RESCUE WORDS (1946). Losing all hope of seeing again, Chen Yinke was intensely mindful of the many classical texts that he could no longer read and study. Ironically, "rescuing words" became his passionate calling after the Communists' victory in 1949, especially in his work on Liu Rushi.

TO MY WIFE (1946). Travel to and from England after the war brought Chen Yinke no good news in terms of medical treatment, only another round of painful separation from his wife and daughters—and also greater penury, since most of their family savings had been invested in old books.

UNBEARABLY VERDANT (1947). The "Boulevard of Eternal Peace" refers to Chang'an Jie, the main axis that runs north-east through central Beijing. This street, which runs along Tiananmen Square, remained a gathering place for political activists during the Cultural Revolution as well as during the Democracy Movement of 1989.

HURRIED OUT OF THE CITY OF NORTHERN PEACE (1948). During the Sino-Japanese War, China's capital was renamed Beiping, Northern Peace. During the civil war, Chen Yinke had to flee the north and was especially reluctant to part with his friend, the historian Fu Sinian (1896-1950).

WARNING (1949). Xi Wang Mu, Queen Mother of the West, is a Chinese goddess especially prominent in Daoist temples. Her name reveals her most important characteristics: she is royal, female and is associated with the lands to the West of China's borders (Tibet and India). The Queen Mother of the West was described as the dispenser of prosperity and longevity—precisely what China's people longed for and what they would sacrifice most dramatically during the reign of Mao Zedong, which started with the Communist takeover in 1949.

ON THE SEVENTH DAY OF THE SEVENTH MONTH (1949). Chen Yinke and his wife Tang Yun were accustomed to exchanging poems on this occasion known as Qixi Festival (literally "The Night of Sevens"). Traditionally, a woman would demonstrate her domestic arts on this day by carving a melon signifying hopes for a good husband. Here, Chen voices his own wishes for domestic tranquility at a time when China was already in the throes of a violent transition, which he feared would bring even worse atrocities in its wake.

BOMBING (1950). During the winter months of 1950, Jiang Kai-shek's Nationalist air force fought its last battles against the Communists in Canton. One of the worst air raids took place in February during the Spring Festival which marks the start of a new lunar year.

DREAMS (1951). Unable to actually visit his family's graves, Chen Yinke was filled with longing for their ancestral place in Yining, Jiangxi. As a man who could not honor his ancestors, Chen suffered from loneliness, despite the scholarly refuge he had found (for a while) at Sun Yatsen University in Canton.

AFTERLIFE (1953). Stalin's death in March 1953 coincided with the Communist Party's propaganda about "victory" in the Korean War. By this time, Chen Yinke had become a seasoned disbeliever in official propaganda.

BLIND MAN'S CANE (1954). Chinese folk tales and Daoist mythology often dwell on some magical weapon which a sage uses to combat the evils of the world. Chen Yinke did not see himself as either a sage or a folk hero. Rather, by 1954, his blindness had opened a fresh window onto China's "calamities"—which included tens of thousands of peasants killed or maimed in Mao Zedong's land reform campaigns. These campaigns were touted as a great success by some of Chen's own academic colleagues and students eager for the Party's approval.

HEROES (1955). The more public propaganda heralded the glories of land reform and of the Soviet style Five Year Plan, the more gloomy Chen Yinke became. Not even historical studies seemed to offer guidance, or solace.

POEMS ENOUGH FOR MY BEHEADING (1956). In the fall of this year, the eminent scholar Zhang Shizhao (1881-1973) came to Canton to persuade Chen Yinke once again to move north and to serve as Director of the Party's History Institute. Chen refused, leaving Zhang impressed with Chen Yinke's ethical standards and his domestic tranquility in difficult times. "Winter plum" was Chen's often-used metaphor for his wife.

CAWING (1957). In the spring of 1957, Mao Zedong launched the "Hundred Flowers Campaign," supposedly to encourage intellectuals to speak out about the Communists' rule. From the inception of this campaign, Chen was pessimistic about the Party's ultimate goal. Within a few months, his dark suspicions were confirmed by the "Anti-Rightist" movement, which punished all who had dared to criticize the excesses of the regime. Often Chen referred to Party authorities as fake "immortals."

OLD KNOTS (1957). In traditional Chinese painting, bamboo was a symbol of the virtuous scholar who managed to withstand the chill winds of political adversity.

A PRISONER OF RUSH-LEAF SWORDS (1957). "Waves from Hunan" evokes the birthplace of Mao Zedong, who was the driving force behind both the "Hundred Flowers Campaign" and the "Anti-Rightist" crackdown that followed. Chen Yinke managed to keep his personal distance from both events, but clearly intuited their brutal impact upon China's population, and the fact that he would not be able to stay above the fray of politics much longer. By 1958-59, he had become a target of a campaign against "too much history" at his own university in Canton.

MOURNING FOR LANGUAGE AND LAND (1962). Liu Rushi's lover (and later husband) was Qian Qianyi (1582–1664) a noted Ming dynasty official, scholar and historian who used the studio name of "Master of Crimson Clouds." As a Ming loyalist, Qian became a prominent target and was arrested by the Manchu invaders when they conquered China in 1644. He died in prison. Liu Rishi committed suicide shortly thereafter.

A CHILLING SPRING (1963). Both cranes and unicorns are symbols of enlightened moral rule in the Confucian cannon. Their departure signals social chaos.

DIVINATION (1963). One year before the prophecy depicted in this poem, Mao Zedong launched his "Socialist Education Campaign" to root out potential "reactionaries" in public life. Chen Yinke, already attacked in 1958-59, had found refuge in silence and in his book about Liu Rushi. By 1963, Chen sensed that the political situation was going to get much worse for him, and for China. For a brief time, he was still able to "shutter the gate," keeping the howls of dogmatism at bay. The outbreak of the Cultural Revolution in 1966 confirmed his worst fears.

SOLITARY STALK (1964). Hollyhock was a symbol linked to an ancient concubine, who died shortly after being chosen as a favorite by the Emperor Wu of the Han dynasty. Having already identified with several tragic female figures, Chen Yinke extracted more and more of them from historical tales as he sought to prepare himself for the dark days that seemed to be coming in the winter of 1964.

THE SKULL OF MERCY (1964). As a historian of Buddhism, Chen was intimately familiar with Indian scholarship on the evolution of sacred texts. Cut off from other researchers, both Chinese and foreign, he imagined the physical remains of the Buddha, as well as the ethical value of compassion, safe in some place "west" of China—which most often referred to India and Tibet.

ONE GAUNT BRUSH (1964). The scroll that inspired this poem had belonged to Tang Jingsong (1841–1903), the scholarly grandfather of Chen Yinke's wife, Tang Yun. Like Chen's own ancestors, Tang Jingsong had sought to serve the Qing dynasty with honor. First as a commander during the Sino-French War (1884-1883) and later as governor of Taiwan, he discovered that China's rulers did not share his moral values. As Chen Yinke faced the decimation of the 1960s, Tang Jinsong's earlier efforts to bring ethics into the public realm gained tragic significance. "Tears of lead" was a common Confucian expression for the sorrows of a disillusioned scholar. "Mulberry fields swallowed by black seas" is a metaphor often used to convey catastrophic upheavals in Confucian historiography.

A PILFERED LIFE AMONG THE GRASSES (1964). Having become a target of political attacks in 1958-1959, Chen Yinke expected the worst during Mao's "Socialist Education Campaign." Earlier, he had been accused of being too embedded in the past. Now, he prepared for being pilloried simply for his writing skills. In fact, this turned out to be a realistic premonition, since the Red Guards during the Cultural Revolution denounced anyone who had been "privileged" with a classical education or with study abroad. Chen was an ideal victim on both counts.

PEONY MARKET (1965). As a new lunar year dawned in the winter of 1965, Chen Yinke's premonitions about cultural destruction grew more acute. Canton's raucous flower market is used in this poem as a contrast to his quiet affection for Tang Yun, his "winter plum," as well as to the lost symbolism of the peony ("The King of Flowers"), which used to suggest nobility of character.

COMMON FOLK BECOME MURDEROUS (1966). The outbreak of the Cultural Revolution in Beijing rapidly engulfed the streets of Canton as well. High school students and ordinary workers were the first to rush into the ranks of the Maoist Red Guards in order to attack prominent teachers and party officials. Chen Yinke bemoaned their naïveté even before they came to attack him personally. He had glimpsed murder in their eyes and saw how they had fallen pray to simplistic propaganda about legends such as that of Monkey King, Sun Wukong. Once portrayed as a guardian of Buddhist teachings, Sun was now painted as an avaricious "proletarian" rebel ready to feast on stolen fruit.

THE DAY I SHOULD HAVE SWEPT FAMILY GRAVES (1967). With the start of the lunar New Year in 1967, Chen Yinke's gloom deepened. The attacks on him grew more violent; his wife lay ill, and there was no hope of visiting family graves on the traditional Qing Ming Festival—a time that also used to recall the legend of Jie Zhitui, a virtuous official who had refused to serve with his prince's hypocritical sycophants. After burning down a forest and killing the self-exiled Jie, the prince became regretful and ordered that no warm food be served during the three days of the Qing Ming Festival.

TRAPPED IN AN OCEAN OF RED SLOGANS (1967). Less than a year after the start of the Cultural Revolution, Canton's Red Guards turned their violent attention to Chen Yinke. Ashamed of his debilitating weakness and hunger ("this rice-begging body") and unable to counter false accusations, the blind historian continued to worry about the evil effects of the idolatrous worship of Mao Zedong upon China's public life.

FUNERAL ORATION FOR MY WIFE, BEFORE SHE LEAVES (1968). Tang Yun's worsening health caused Chen Yinke greater worry than the vicious attacks heaped upon him by the Red Guards. As his despair deepened, he turned to grim examples from China's historical legends. The Han dynasty scholar Wang Zhang was supposed to have been so destitute that he lay ill with no covering but a thin blanket used to cover oxen. Wang spent his nights sobbing and trembling from the cold. His only comfort was his wife, whose tears somehow kept the bitter rains from gnawing Wang Zhang to death. Eventually he recovered and was promoted as a virtuous official by the emperor—a fate whose tragic irony weighed upon Chen Yinke's troubled mind during the last year of his life. The "nine rivers of hell" figure prominently in Daoist and Buddhist mythology.

SAME DREAM, SAME MIRROR (1945-1960). Chen Yinke's wife, Tang Yun, was an accomplished poet in the classical style. Each year, on their wedding anniversary, the couple would exchange poems that would embroider certain words in each other's verses. In the mid 1940s, their "flight of swallows" (a reference to their three young daughters) appeared safe. Later, illness and sorrow become a dominant theme. The italicized lines are meant to convey Tang Yun's voice.

ABOUT THE AUTHOR

Vera Schwarcz was born and raised in Cluj, Romania, where she began her explorations of poetry in several languages. Her mother tongues include Hungarian and Romanian, with Yiddish, German, Hebrew, Russian and French added along the way. After emigrating to the United States in 1962, she pursued degrees in East Asian studies and history at Vassar, Yale and Stanford. A member of the first group of exchange scholars to be sent to China in the spring of 1979, she has returned to Beijing repeatedly during the past three decades. All along, her corpus of scholarly writing has been accompanied by the publication of poems in several languages in the United States, Europe and Asia. The daughter of Holocaust survivors, Schwarcz has made the quest for remembrance a central theme in all her works. Her writing has been nominated for the National Jewish Book Award and has been accorded several major grants, including a Guggenheim Fellowship. She holds the Freeman Chair in East Asian Studies at Wesleyan University. Vera Schwarcz lives in West Hartford, Connecticut.

This book is set in Garamond Premier Pro, which had its genesis in 1988 when type-designer Robert Slimbach visited the Plantin-Moretus Museum in Antwerp, Belgium, to study its collection of Claude Garamond's metal punches and typefaces. During the mid-fifteen hundreds, Garamond—a Parisian punch-cutter—produced a refined array of book types that combined an unprecedented degree of balance and elegance, for centuries standing as the pinnacle of beauty and practicality in type-founding. Slimbach has created an entirely new interpretation based on Garamond's designs and on compatible italics cut by Robert Granjon, Garamond's contemporary.

To order additional copies of this book
or other Antrim House titles, contact the publisher at

Antrim House
21 Goodrich Rd., Simsbury, CT 06070
860.217.0023, AntrimHouse@comcast.net
or the house website (www.AntrimHouseBooks.com).

•

On the house website
in addition to information on books
you will find sample poems, upcoming events,
and a "seminar room" featuring supplemental biography,
notes, images, poems, reviews, and
writing suggestions.